COMFORT FOR YOUR HEART

When the holidays hurt

SPECIAL SERIES WORKBOOK

25-Day Companion for Surviving the Season When You're Grieving or Dealing with Loss

RENEE WOOD, MSW

Copyright © 2025 by Renee Wood, MSW

All rights reserved. No part of this publication may be reproduced, stored in a retrieval system, or transmitted in any form or by any means—electronic, mechanical, photocopying, recording, or otherwise—without the prior written permission of the publisher, except in the case of brief quotations embodied in critical reviews, articles, or scholarly works.

Medical disclaimer: This workbook provides general emotional-wellness information and is not a substitute for professional mental-health care.

For permission requests, please contact:
info@gentlenudges.com
Printed in the United States of America
First Edition
ISBN: 979-8-9991939-6-4
Cover & Interior Design: Gentle Nudges Press
Compiled and Edited by: Renee Wood, MSW
Published by: Gentle Nudges Press

*For those who know the holidays
will be different this year.*

This journal belongs to:

_____

"Each one of us has to find our way into that middle ground. A place that doesn't ask us to deny our grief and one that doesn't doom us forever."
~Megan Devine

This is where we begin

This season is hard. There's no other way to say it. The world wants you to be merry and bright, but you're just trying to survive until January.

The holiday music isn't helping. The empty chair at the table isn't hypothetical, it's brutally, painfully real.

Here's what I want you to know: You don't have to do this season 'right.' There is no right. There's only what you can bear, and what you can't. There's only showing up for yourself with the tenderness you'd want for anyone else in your shoes.

These 25 days of guided pages aren't here to fix you or rush you through your grief. They're here to be a place to visit when you need a break. To remind you that you're not alone in this tender, terrible place. To offer you permission to feel everything, to skip the things that hurt too much, to find small mercies in the middle of it all.

Use these pages however you need. Read ahead if you want. Skip a day if you must. Scribble in the margins or tear them up if it helps. This work, and this workbook is yours.

Let's get through this together.

Very Warmly,

Renee

Table of Contents

DAY 1: Permission to Not Be Okay 10

DAY 2: Your Emotional Weather Report...............12

You're Not Losing Your Mind:
Holiday Grief Checklist 14

DAY 3: When Resistance Makes It Harder...........18

DAY 4: Let Your Grief Show..20

DAY 5: Name What You Feel 22

DAY 6: Go Easy on Yourself 24

DAY 7: *The Art of Saying No* 26

DAY 8: Do It Your Way 28

DAY 9: Guilt is Optional 30

DAY 10: Bring Them Along 32

DAY 11: You Can Be Mad..34

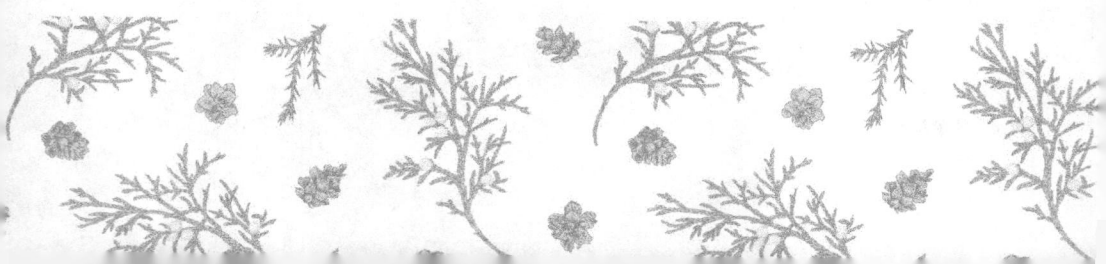

DAY 12: When People Say the Wrong Thing 36

DAY 13: Let Their Life Show Up Too 38

DAY 14: The Relief of Low Expectations 40

DAY 15: When People Grieve Differently 42

DAY 16: Keep Them Close 44

DAY 17: Acknowledge the Empty Seat 46

DAY 18: Protecting Your Grief.. 48

DAY 19: Write Them a Letter 50

DAY 20: Find Your People.. 52

DAY 21: Change Your Scenery..54

DAY 22: Missing Who You Were 56

DAY 23: Solitude vs. Isolation...58

DAY 24: When Grief and Joy Collide....................... 60

DAY 25: All is Welcome Here...62

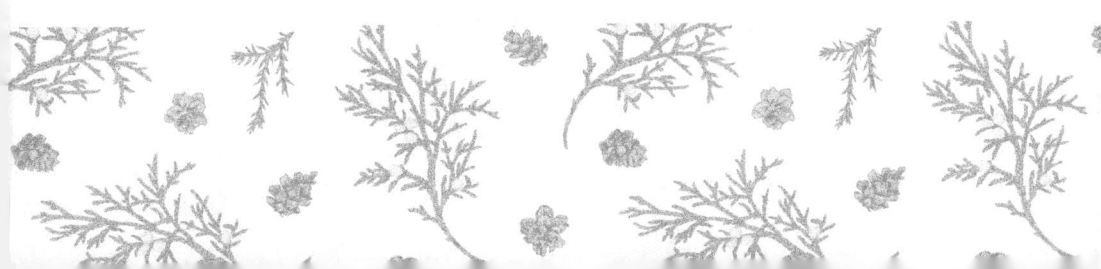

DAY 1

Permission to Not Be Okay

Grief doesn't come with manners. It barges in and throws you down but doesn't offer to help you up. One minute it respects your space and keeps a polite distance; the next, it's all over you and there's no escape.

The world is draped in tinsel and joy, and here you are, carrying a heart that's been shattered and weighs a million pounds. That's not a character flaw—that's called being human in the middle of loss.

The bravest thing you can do today is let your grief show up without apologizing for it. You don't need to put on a happy face. You don't need to explain why you can't muster enthusiasm for "Silent Nights" or why the sight of twinkling lights feels like a boot to the chest.

Your grief is not a social inconvenience—it's the evidence of deep love. And love, even in its most painful form, deserves to be honored, not hidden.

Some days you'll cry at Hallmark Channel trailers; other days you'll feel strangely fine. Both are welcome. The world may be sparkly on the outside, but inside you, the darkness asks only this: tell the truth about how you are and keep breathing through the days as they pass.

What fear keeps you from showing your true feelings today? If you allowed your grief to be seen, how would the day be different?

Today, you have permission to be exactly as okay or not-okay as you are.

DAY 2

Your Emotional Weather Report

You can do everything "right" and still get taken out by something you never saw coming. Kind of like checking both ways for cars before crossing the street and then getting hit by a plane.

Sometimes the dread of what's coming is worse than the day itself. The anticipatory anxiety—watching the calendar pages flip closer, seeing decorations multiply in stores, counting down the days—can be its own special form of torture. You're bracing for impact, but you don't know when or how hard it'll hit.

One minute you're laughing with friends; the next, you're undone when it's time to take a picture they should have been in but won't be.

This isn't you losing your mind. This is grief doing what grief does. It doesn't keep a schedule or care that you've promised you'd hold it together. It just shows up unannounced—an uninvited guest who sucks the oxygen out of the room and refuses to leave.

The emotional roller coaster doesn't mean you're doing it wrong. It means you're doing it right—you're feeling the fullness of life without turning to stone. There's no "getting over" it, only learning to move forward with what remains.

When the dips come—and they will—let them stand as measures of love, not just reminders of loss.

Think back to a time when a wave of emotion caught you off guard. How did you respond to yourself in that moment? What are you dreading most about the days ahead?

_____

_____

_____

_____

_____

_____

_____

_____

_____

_____

_____

_____

_____

_____

_____

_____

_____

_____

_____

_____

Meet each change in your emotional storm with curiosity and compassion, not criticism.

You're Not Losing Your Mind: Holiday Grief Checklist

Here's the thing about grief during the holidays: it might make you do and feel things that seem completely unhinged.

Until you realize that literally everyone who's grieving does the exact same things. So, here's a list of "normal grief" habits.

Check what applies—not to keep score, but because sometimes you just need to know you're not the only one dealing with a dark kaleidoscope of emotions.

☐ Cried in public when a holiday song came on

☐ Felt bitter seeing other people's holiday cards

☐ Said no to every single invitation

☐ Said yes to something, then cancelled last minute

☐ Put up decorations, then regretted it

☐ Couldn't bring yourself to decorate at all

☐ Did all your shopping online to avoid the cheer

☐ Abandoned your cart in the middle of the store

☐ Felt guilty for having one moment that didn't hurt

☐ Wished you fall asleep and wake up in January

☐ Argued about keeping or changing a tradition

☐ Felt actual relief when an event got cancelled

☐ Had to leave somewhere earlier than you planned

☐ Bought holiday cards but never sent them

☐ Got resentful seeing happy people

☐ Scrolled past every holiday post on social media

☐ Burst into tears (In public, naturally)

☐ Said "I'm fine" when you definitely were not fine

☐ Had that flash where you forgot for a second

☐ Almost called their number

☐ Felt jealous of people who still have their person

☐ Someone told you "They're in a better place"

☐ Were told "they wouldn't want you to be sad"

☐ Hugged something that was theirs

☐ Talked to them out loud

☐ Asked them to send you a sign

☐ Had someone unexpected come through for you

☐ Made a new friend who's also in "the club"

(Dead parent club, widow club, dead child club)

☐ Can't relate to some old friends anymore

☐ Had that awkward moment when someone who didn't know asked about them

☐ Stayed in bed all day

If you checked:

0-10 boxes: You're normal.
11-20 boxes: You're normal.
20-300 boxes: You're normal.

You're not losing your mind. You're grieving during the holidays. And that looks messy and strange and completely unhinged sometimes.

And you're doing it exactly right.

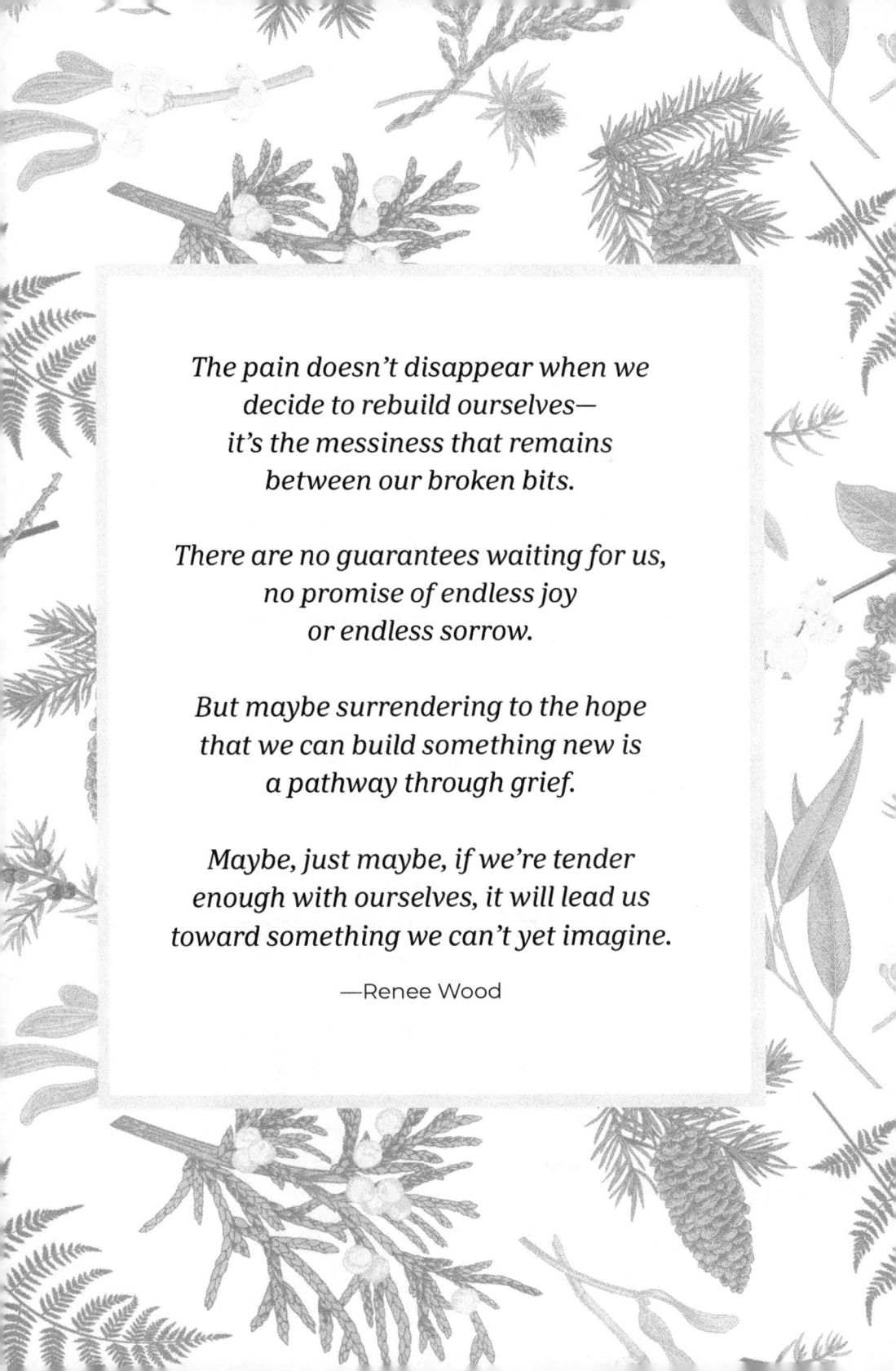

The pain doesn't disappear when we
decide to rebuild ourselves—
it's the messiness that remains
between our broken bits.

There are no guarantees waiting for us,
no promise of endless joy
or endless sorrow.

But maybe surrendering to the hope
that we can build something new is
a pathway through grief.

Maybe, just maybe, if we're tender
enough with ourselves, it will lead us
toward something we can't yet imagine.

—Renee Wood

DAY 3

When Resistance Makes It Harder

Your body knows before your mind does. Tight jaw. Chest so heavy you can't get a full breath. Exhausted but unable to sleep—or sleeping all the time and still feeling wrecked. Heart pounding for no reason.

Grief isn't something you can strong-arm into submission. You can't white-knuckle yourself into feeling okay.

Because the more you try to push grief away, the more it digs in its heels. The more you tell yourself you should be over it by now, the heavier it gets.

What if you loosened your grip? Not on them—but on the fight. On the need to control how you feel, when you cry, how much it hurts.

This doesn't mean giving up. It means giving into what is so you save that energy for actually getting through the day.

Letting go looks different for everyone: Crying until there's nothing left. Saying out loud, "This is terrible and I hate it." Relaxing your shoulders. Taking one full breath.

You don't have to surrender to despair to stop fighting reality.

Where in your body are you holding tension right now? Put your hand there. What are you trying to control your grief in this season that you actually can't control? What if you stopped trying just for an hour?

_____

_____

_____

_____

_____

_____

_____

_____

_____

_____

_____

_____

_____

_____

_____

_____

_____

_____

*What you stop fighting
can't overpower you.*

DAY 4

Let Your Grief Show

You don't owe anyone cheerful camouflage. The pressure to sparkle through the season is relentless, but clarity is kind. Being honest with others—not just with yourself, but with the people around you—about where you actually are is a tender way to move through the holidays.

Watching others feel the spirit of the season while yours remains broken can feel like too heavy a lift. That's fair. But it's also your story this year. And sometimes, the kindest thing you can do is let others in on it.

When you let your grief be visible, you give permission for honesty to exist around you. It might even invite someone else's truth to the table. Love isn't diminished by sorrow; it's revealed through it. So if your eyes brim over at dinner, that's just love remembering out loud.

People might not know what to say. Some will say nothing at all, and that silence can sting. But your grief still deserves to be acknowledged. Saying, "I really miss them," is such a beautiful truth. Real love is strong enough to be seen weeping.

Where are you hiding your grief for others' comfort? What's an honest sentence you could say to someone about how you're really doing?

*When you say what hurts,
it helps.*

DAY 5

Name What You Feel

Emotions are live wires. When you put words to them—lonely, anxious, numb, furious, tender, unmoored—something shifts. They stop being this massive fog you're lost in and become specific things you can have perspective on.

Not "I'm a mess," but "I'm feeling overwhelmed about Christmas Eve." Not "everything is wrong," but "I'm angry that they're not here."

Naming an emotion creates breathing distance. You're not the grief—you're the person experiencing grief. And that tiny bit of space? That's where compassion slips in.

It also shrinks the monster. What's vague and nameless feels huge, but once you say, "This is loneliness," it becomes recognizable. You've felt lonely before. Maybe not this intensely, but you know what it is and what it needs.

You can say "I'm lonely" and know loneliness needs connection. You can say "I'm furious" and know that fury needs release—pound a pillow, scream in the car, hit the pavement for a power walk.

So, name your emotions today—not to analyze them or fix them, but to understand what you need.

Which emotions best describe what you're feeling today? What do these feelings need and how can you take to meet that need?

> · Exhausted · Bitter · Relieved · Guilty · Numb · Panicky
> · Tender · Raw · Resentful · Undone · Hollow · Restless
> · Abandoned · Fragile · Furious · Sad · Anxious ·
> Overwhelmed · Empty · Betrayed · Lost · Afraid ·
> Hopeless · Weary · Gutted

*When you name the ache,
you know how to soothe it.*

DAY 6

Go Easy on Yourself

Grief exhausts every system: mind, body, spirit. The errands, the texts, the expectations—they'll all keep calling. But today, what if you called a truce with yourself? Lower the bar until it's kindness-shaped. Let the bed stay unmade, the inbox wait, the tears come.

You're carrying something invisible and heavy; it's okay to rest under the weight of it. Rest isn't quitting—it's necessary maintenance. The world can manage without your constant caretaking for a little while. You don't have to be strong every minute of every day. You don't have to keep it together for everyone else.

Grace begins the moment you stop demanding more strength than you have. The moment you say, 'This is all I can do today, and it's enough.' Give yourself the same mercy you'd give to anyone else you love who's hurting this much.

Maybe today that looks like: staying in pajamas until noon. Ordering takeout instead of cooking. Canceling the thing you said you'd do. Taking a nap at 2pm. Crying in the shower. Watching something mindless on TV. Whatever your body and heart are asking for.

Where have you been pushing yourself to 'keep it together'? What are three specific, small acts of caring for yourself you can do today?

_____
_____
_____
_____
_____
_____
_____
_____
_____
_____
_____
_____
_____
_____
_____
_____
_____

*You don't have to earn rest.
You just have to take it.*

DAY 7

The Art of Saying No

You can't heal if you're worried about other people's comfort. The truth is: every invitation, every tradition, every gathering—it's all optional. Even the ones you already said yes to.

Let your calendar reflect your capacity, not your guilt. You're in charge of protecting your energy and your heart.

Even when you think you can handle something, you might discover in the moment that you can't. So have two plans: the hopeful one and the escape plan. Maybe you'll stay the whole evening. Maybe you'll leave after twenty minutes. Whatever you choose is fine.

Know your exit strategy before walking in. A time limit or an emotional cue. Then honor it without apology.

You can leave your cart mid-aisle. Slip out without goodbye. Turn your car around. Say "I need to leave now"—even if you just arrived.

This isn't rudeness. It's self-grace. You are knowing yourself well enough to honor what you can and cannot bear. Allowing yourself to change your mind, even at the last minute.

Which event or expectation already feels like too much? How would it feel to make a commitment to yourself to make guilt-free decisions this year?

_____
_____
_____
_____
_____
_____
_____
_____
_____
_____
_____
_____
_____
_____
_____
_____
_____
_____
_____
_____
_____

*Setting boundaries is
self-compassion in action.*

DAY 8

Do It Your Way

Every store and commercial will try to sell you their version of "holiday spirit." Don't buy it. Create the season that fits your current heart, not your past one.

Maybe you will decorate one small corner instead of the whole house. Maybe you stay in pajamas and order takeout. You're still participating in life—just in a way that feels manageable.

Traditions can be both comforting and cruel. If the old ways hurt this year, try new ones. Skip midnight Mass and watch a movie instead. Volunteer at a food bank. Donate a book to your library that reminds you of them. Love evolves; so can rituals.

Make room for what feels meaningful—or simply what feels possible—and let the rest go without guilt. Redefining what matters is its own kind of gift, and this year, it's the one your healing heart needs the most.

Which tradition would you still want to keep? Either as it was or by creating a new version. Is there a new ritual you want to begin?

*Peace often arrives through
quiet reinvention.*

DAY 9

Guilt is Optional

Guilt is grief's loudest companion. Guilt that you're not handling it better. Guilt that you're burdening others. Guilt that you laughed today, or didn't call your friend back, or that you're somehow failing at this impossible thing called loss.

The truth is: there is no failing at grief. There's no way to do it wrong. You're not too much, and you're not too little.

You're not moving too slowly or healing too fast. You're simply in it—doing the only thing anyone can do—surviving it one next right baby step at a time.

Guilt wants you to believe you should be different than you are. NOT that you are exactly where you need to be.

Guilt is optional. So put it down. Do it now.

Make a list of the guilt you are carrying about your grieving. What would it feel like to set that heaviness down, even just for today?

_____
_____
_____
_____
_____
_____
_____
_____
_____
_____
_____
_____
_____
_____
_____
_____
_____
_____

***Guilt has never changed
an outcome in your favor.***

DAY 10

Bring Them Along

Grief will try to convince you that joy and remembrance can't coexist—but they can. The season may look different now, but love can still have a seat at the table.

What kind of small ritual of remembrance could bring you comfort? It doesn't have to be elaborate. Maybe it's lighting a special candle each evening—a gentle reminder that their memory still lights your way and warms your heart.

Maybe it's buying or making an ornament that captures something about them—their humor, their love of the ocean, their terrible singing voice. Or placing a favorite photo in a seasonal frame to bring out each year.

Maybe it's wearing something of theirs. Playing their favorite song. Making their recipe just for yourself. Watching the movie they loved. Taking a walk to the place you used to go together.

These aren't acts of pretending they're still here—they're ways of honoring that they were here, that they mattered, and that you are not moving on, but moving forward with them.

What small, private ritual could you create to include your loved one this season? What would feel honoring without being overwhelming?

_____
_____
_____
_____
_____
_____
_____
_____
_____
_____
_____
_____
_____
_____
_____
_____
_____
_____
_____
_____

**You don't have to leave them behind
to keep moving forward.**

DAY 11

You Can Be Mad

Maybe you're not just sad. Maybe you're furious. Furious at the unfairness of it all. Furious at a world that keeps spinning when yours has stopped. Furious at people who complain about minor inconveniences when you'd give anything for one more ordinary day with your person.

Anger is a basic human emotion—alongside fear and sadness. And when those three arrive together, they leave little room for joy or happiness.

But anger isn't all bad. It's intelligent—it rises to defend what was sacred. It tells the truth that something unbearable has happened. Anger doesn't mean you're bitter or broken; it means you're protecting something deeply important.

Anger needs to be expressed, not buried. When you let it move—through words, tears, motion, or sound—it becomes a tunnel you can walk through instead of a cave you stay trapped in.

This pain will never feel like a gift. But when anger begins to soften, it can widen your compassion—for yourself, for others, for this messy, fragile world.

What's something you've been angry about recently? Write it all down—spoken or unspoken, rational or irrational. Justifiable or not.

*Anger is a basic human emotion.
Just like love. Just like joy.*

DAY 12

When People Say the Wrong Thing

'They're in a better place.' 'Everything happens for a reason.' 'At least they're not suffering.' People mean well. They really do. AND sometimes their words absolutely not helpful. In fact, they can be maddening.

You don't have to educate everyone. You don't have to explain why platitudes don't help. You can simply smile and walk away, or you can say, 'I know you mean well, but what I really need right now is...

It's okay to tell people what you actually need: silence, a hug, someone to just sit with you, help with meals for a weekend, a ride to the airport.

Most people are terrified of grief. They don't know what to say, so they reach for something—anything—to fill the silence. Try to remember: their awkwardness isn't about you.

It's about their own discomfort with the reality that life is fragile and loss is inevitable. Forgive them if you can. And protect yourself when you can't.

What have people said that hurt, even if they meant well? What do you actually need to hear instead?

You can forgive people's awkwardness without absorbing their words.

DAY 13

Let Their Life Show Up Too

Their absence will show up at every gathering. The empty chair. The missing laugh. The corny jokes or stories they repeat. You can't avoid that.

But here's what you can choose: to let their life show up too.

Do everything they loved. Make their favorite dessert. Play home videos they're a part of. Wear something they wore.

This isn't pretending they're here. It's refusing to let their absence be the only thing that defines the holidays.

Their life mattered. Their joy mattered. The things they loved and the way they loved them—that doesn't disappear just because they're gone.

You get to decide whether the holidays become a shrine to loss or a celebration of the whole person. Not every minute has to be joyful. But some moments can remember what brought them joy.

Their absence will take up space no matter what you do. But their life can take up space too—if you let it.

What was one thing they loved about the holidays or that you remember them for? How could you bring that into this season?

_____
_____
_____
_____
_____
_____
_____
_____
_____
_____
_____
_____
_____
_____
_____
_____
_____
_____
_____
_____
_____

Just for a day, let their life and love take up more space than you grief.

DAY 14

The Relief of Low Expectations

What if this year, you aimed for 'survived' instead of 'thrived'? What if you gave yourself permission to have the bare minimum holiday season? No elaborate meals. No perfect gifts. No forced cheer. Just... getting through.

There's enormous relief in lowering the bar. When you stop trying to maintain the facade of normal, you create space for what's actually here: grief, yes, but also small moments of rest, tiny glimmers of okay-ness, the radical act of just surviving.

You don't need to make this season special or meaningful or memorable. You just need to make it bearable.

Be still and let yourself off of every hook. Let it all go: the busy, the expectations, the hustle, the habits and sit back and let it all go by.

If you lowered the bar all the way to the ground, what would you actually do this season? What's the absolute minimum?

Sometimes lowering the bar is the best action you can take.

DAY 15

When People Grieve Differently

People grieve in completely different ways. And during the holidays, those differences become impossible to ignore—and easy to judge.

Someone handles their loss by keeping every tradition intact while you want to burn it all down. They talk about their person constantly while you can barely speak their name. They're "doing so well" while you're barely holding on.

None of these is wrong. They're just different.

But your mind makes up stories: You're doing it wrong. Look at them—they're handling it better. You're too much. Or you're not sad enough.

Stop. Your grief doesn't have to look like anyone else's to be valid.

The person who seems to be coping better isn't stronger than you—they're just surviving differently. The person falling apart isn't weaker. The person who won't talk isn't heartless, and the person who can't stop talking isn't "stuck."

You can't control how others grieve. You can only honor what you need—without judging yourself against what others do.

Have you ever compared your grief to anyone else's? Have you noticed differences in how people grieve?

_____
_____
_____
_____
_____
_____
_____
_____
_____
_____
_____
_____
_____
_____
_____
_____
_____
_____
_____
_____

People have different ways of grieving — all of them valid, none of them easy.

DAY 16

Keep Them Close

Sometimes you'll feel them without trying. A song comes on. A butterfly lands beside you. You have a dream so real you want to stay asleep forever.

You don't have to justify these moments or explain them away. If it brings comfort, let it. If it feels like they are reaching back, you're allowed to believe it.

There are also intentional ways to keep them close: wear their watch or ring; listen to a voicemail; carry something small of theirs around with you; play their favorite song; make their favorite meal; read the book they loved.

You aren't living in the past. You're carrying them forward with you.

Some people will understand. Others won't. Some may say you need to "move on." But keeping them close doesn't prevent healing—it can be part of it. Staying connected while learning to live without can be a beautiful lifeline.

You get to decide what keeps you tethered to their love—a photo, an ornament, their handwriting, a ritual, a sign. Whatever works for you is the right thing to do.

What made you feel close to them this week? What's one intentional way you've decided to feel their love close?

_____
_____
_____
_____
_____
_____
_____
_____
_____
_____
_____
_____
_____
_____
_____
_____
_____
_____
_____
_____
_____
_____

*Keeping you close isn't living in the past—
it's how I move forward with you.*

DAY 17

Acknowledge the Empty Seat

The empty chair. The missing voice. The space where they should be sitting, laughing, sharing how they like cornbread stuffing more.

Not talking about who's missing doesn't make you miss them less. It just makes the silence louder.

So, say it out loud. "I miss Dad being here." "Mom would have loved this pie." "This feels weird without them." Simple acknowledgment—that's all it takes.

You don't need an elaborate ritual. Light a candle. Set out their photo. Leave their chair where it always was. Tell their stories. Say their name and bring them into the conversation like you always have.

Not everyone will be comfortable with this. Some family members might resist talking about them at all. That's their grief, not yours.

Your grief doesn't need permission from the room. The absence is real whether you speak it or not. Speaking it just makes the love visible too.

How could you make their absence visible in a public or family setting in a way that feels loving? How can you make space at the table for them without feeling overwhelmed?

*When absence is honored aloud,
it becomes presence remembered.*

DAY 18

Protecting Your Grief

Because of the travel, visiting and celebrating over the holidays, it's likely you'll run into people who aren't as close to your grief.

Some people will be easy to talk to. Others might ask too many questions, offer unhelpful advice, or respond in ways that leave you feeling worse. It's not that they're bad people—it's just that you may not have the energy.

It feels strange to talk around what's actually happening. To answer "We're doing okay" when nothing is okay. To smile through small talk when your heart is breaking. But protecting yourself isn't dishonest. It's discernment.

You get to gauge: Do I have the energy for this conversation today? Will sharing this right now help me or hurt me? Is this the right person, the right moment, the right setting?

Sometimes you'll share openly. Sometimes you'll keep it private. Sometimes you'll tell a complete stranger and withhold from family. All of that is allowed.

Your grief is yours. You get to choose who witnesses it and when—based on what you need, not what others expect.

What's one sentence you can have ready when you're unprepared, unwilling or unable to talk about how your doing?

*Protecting your heart is a necessary
act of love and compassion.*

DAY 19

Write Them a Letter

Sometimes words meant for them still linger inside you—heavy, unfinished, unspoken. Write them down. Tell them what you miss, what you noticed today, the ordinary details they would have understood. Tell them about the mundane things—the weather, how you feel today, the small moment that made you think of them.

This isn't about being heard; it's about releasing what's pressing against your chest. It's about giving words to what love still needs to say. Writing keeps the conversation going, even when they can't answer back. It's one way to let love keep moving—to let it find expression, even now. Because love doesn't end when life does.

What would you want your loved one to know about your life today? Tell them the things you're proud of yourself for.

*Writing isn't just an expression of love;
one day it will be your evidence of healing.*

DAY 20

Find Your People

Grief is lonely. Even surrounded by people who love you, it can still feel isolating. The world moves on and people may seem ready for you to move on, too.

But then there are the people who get it. The ones you never expected who can stand unwavering as a witness to your pain.

Sometimes the right people find you, but sometimes you need to find your people. The best way to do this is to be practical and honest about what you need and saying it out loud.

"I need people who won't tell me things happen for a reason." "I need people who let me talk about them." "I need some practical help right now—can you bring dinner Thursday?"

Most people want to help, but still need to be told what's helpful. You don't have to carry this alone. Grief support groups exist—online and in person. People who speak your language without you having to translate.

Finding them starts with admitting you need them. And then asking.

Write a "help wanted ad" for the kind of support you actually need right now. Be specific. Be honest. What qualities are you looking for? What would they do (or not do)?

Example:

HELP WANTED: In search of someone who can be on call 24/7 for long talks, quick chats, and everything in between. Must be willing to listen to me say the same things over and over and feel no urgency to "fix" me.

Bonus points if you've been through this and won't tell me "it gets better" or "time heals all wounds." Comfortable with silence, tears, and occasional rage required.

_____
_____
_____
_____
_____
_____
_____
_____
_____
_____
_____
_____
_____

Grief is lonely.
But you don't have to be.

DAY 21

Change Your Scenery

Sometimes the house feels like it's closing in and the grief is stuck within the walls of every room. During the holidays, it gets worse and it may feel good to go someplace else. Anywhere else.

This doesn't have to be dramatic. Changing your scenery can be as simple as going to a different coffee shop. Taking a drive to a park you've never been to. Walking a different route. Anywhere that isn't steeped with the life that used to contain them.

The point isn't to run from your grief. It's to give yourself a break from the environment where grief takes up all the space. To interrupt the patterns. To let your nervous system experience something different, even for a few hours.

Nature helps. If you can get outside—even for ten minutes—do it. Fresh air on your face. Trees that don't care about Christmas. The steadiness of the earth. The world is bigger than your grief, and sometimes you need to be reminded of that.

Sometimes seeing the world through a different lens lets you live in a different reality, even if just for a moment.

Where could you go today, this week, or this season that might feel easier than home? A place with no memories attached—just neutral ground where grief doesn't live on every corner.

List 3 places (realistic or far-fetched):

_____
_____
_____
_____
_____
_____
_____
_____
_____
_____
_____
_____
_____
_____
_____
_____

Grief may live in you, but you can take breaks from living in grief.

DAY 22

Missing Who You Were

This season isn't just about missing them. Sometimes it's about missing who you used to be too.

Grief changes more than your days—it changes you. You may feel like the holidays will never be happy again. You may feel like you'll never feel lighthearted again—or that any good feelings will always be served with a chaser of guilt.

You're grieving two losses, so it's ok to feel off balance as you learn to carry what can't be fixed.

You're becoming someone different: Not better. Not worse. Just different. More aware of life's fragility. Less patient with nonsense. More attuned to what actually matters.

Grief changed you, and you don't have to like the changes. You don't have to be grateful for what loss has taught you.

And you can still allow your heart to expand big enough to carry both love and grief together.

What parts of your old self do you find yourself missing the most? (Optimism? Your ability to enjoy small things? Your lightness?)

_____
_____
_____
_____
_____

What's one quality you've gained (even unwillingly) through grief? (Resilience? Deeper compassion? Less tolerance for BS?)

_____
_____
_____
_____
_____
_____
_____
_____
_____

I don't have to be grateful for what loss taught me.

DAY 23

Solitude vs. Isolation

There's a difference between choosing to be alone and being overcome by loneliness.

Solitude is restorative: the relief of not performing or worrying about other people's comfort around you.

Isolation is dangerous: the belief that you're a burden, that your grief is "too much."

During the holidays, both can feel necessary—and both can be risky. You need time alone to let your guard down. But too much time alone, and the loneliness get heavier.

Grief often nudges you to isolate when what you actually need is connection.

Check in: Am I alone because I need peace, or because I believe I have to be?

Solitude feels like sanctuary. Isolation feels like punishment.

If it's isolation, reach out—text, a grief group, a support forum. Small connections count.

If it's solitude, that's okay—just time-box it: "Today I'm alone; tomorrow I'll check in."

If you're isolating: who is one person you could reach out to? What's one small way you could connect?

_____

_____

_____

_____

_____

_____

_____

If you need solitude: what does restorative alone time look like for you? How will you know when it's time to reconnect?

_____

_____

_____

_____

_____

_____

_____

_____

_____

I respect the days I need rest and honor I need to reach out.

DAY 24

When Grief and Joy Collide

It's ok to let joy and grief coexist. You can miss them desperately and still enjoy your coffee. You can wish they were here and still laugh at something funny. You can carry profound sadness and still feel grateful for small pleasures.

The holidays will hand you these collisions constantly. A moment of connection, immediately followed by the ache of who's missing. A beautiful song that makes you cry and also brings peace. The weird relief of surviving a hard day, mixed with guilt for feeling relief.

It's okay to be thankful, grateful, and grieving all at the same time. Your grief doesn't require constant suffering to prove its real. Your love doesn't require constant pain to prove its depth. They would want you to have the good moments.

When joy shows up—and it will, in small surprising ways—let it. You don't have to hold onto it or make it mean anything. Just let it be there alongside everything else. Both/And. Not Either/Or.

I'm grieving:

_____

_____

I'm grateful for:

_____

_____

I hate that:

_____

_____

I'm thankful for:

_____

_____

It hurts that:

_____

_____

It helps that:

_____

_____

My grief is big but my love is bigger.

DAY 25

All is Welcome Here

Your grief is yours alone—no one else carries your exact ache, shaped by your unique love and relationship.

But you are not alone in grieving.

There are others—though you don't always see them—who also feel out of step with the season. People whose hearts feel heavier than they can hold. People trying to fill a day that still ends in emptiness, no matter what.

You're not a bad person if you just want this day to be over. And you're also allowed to feel a sense of ease if today was gentler than you expected.

You belong to a quiet choir of the brokenhearted who are still here—doing their best to survive one hard day, and then get through the next.

You've lived through another season you weren't sure you could. That's no small miracle.

Let this day be exactly what you need—staying in, reaching out, curling up or breaking down.

All of you is welcome here.

What tangible or doable gift you will give to yourself—something you can bring into the new year? Maybe it's a new habit, a helpful app, music lessons, ear buds.

Decide today: *write it down, download it, set it up, order it or ask for help to make it happen.*

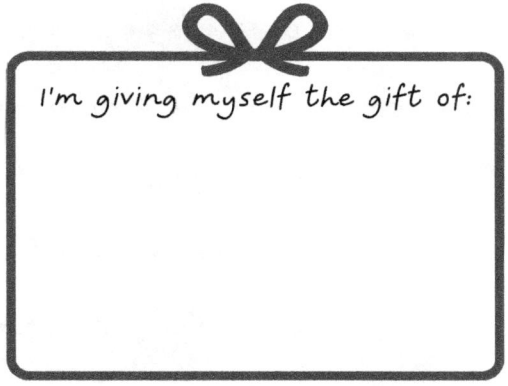

I'm choosing this gift because:

_____
_____
_____
_____
_____
_____
_____
_____
_____

*May you find of peace in the chaos,
light in the darkness, and hope in the midst of grief.*

Maybe your heart was broken this year. Or maybe it's been cracked for a while. Maybe you've started stitching your life together again or maybe you're still unraveling. No matter what, you're still here— you are living proof that love cannot be erased by sorrow. You should be proud of yourself for making it through this year. And even if Christmas is different this year,

Merry Christmas Anyway.

I'm so glad you are prioritizing taking care of yourself. If this book helped make the holidays even the smallest bit more bearable, I'd be so grateful if you'd leave a review on Amazon.

Please share anything you feel might support the next grieving heart who finds this book.

Reviews tell Amazon that **grief support matters** and helps this journal show up for others who may feel misunderstood in their grief.

Need more support?
You may love *How to Heal From Grief Workbook for Women: 12-Week Grief Journal with Prompts to Heat at Your Own Pace and Gently Rebuild Your Life.*